Study Guide and Workbook

The Let Them Theory by Mel Robbins (Daily Summary)

Daily Summary

The purpose of this Study Guide and Workbook is to provide supplemental educational material. It is not intended as a substitute for or replacement of the original source text or materials.

ISBN: 978-1-300-39377-1

Author: Daily Summary

Book Title: Study Guide and Workbook: The Let Them Theory by Mel Robbins (Daily Summary)

TABLE OF CONTENTS

Introduction

In *The Let Them Theory*, Mel Robbins teaches us a radical yet simple truth: **You cannot control others, but you can always control how you respond.** This philosophy—**"Let Them" and "Let Me"**—empowers you to release frustration, reclaim your peace, and take charge of your happiness by focusing on what truly matters: **your choices, your boundaries, and your life.**

Why This Study Guide?

This book is designed to help you **absorb, apply, and internalize** Robbins' lessons through:

- **Daily Summaries:** Concise recaps of key concepts to reinforce learning.

- **Guided Exercises:** Reflective prompts, real-world challenges, and actionable steps to practice the *Let Them Theory* in your daily life.

- **Workbook Sections:** Space to journal, track progress, and solidify your mindset shifts.

Whether you're navigating relationships, career challenges, or personal growth, this guide will help you **stop wasting energy on what you can't change** and start investing in **what you can.**

How to Use This Book

1. **Read the Daily Summaries** – Each section distills Robbins' wisdom into digestible insights.

2. **Complete the Exercises** – Apply the theory through reflection questions and real-life experiments.

3. **Track Your Growth** – Use the workbook pages to document breakthroughs and challenges.

By the end, you'll have more than just knowledge—you'll have **a new way of living**: one where you **let go of control** over others and **step into your power** with confidence.

Your *Let Them* journey starts now. **Let Me** guide you through it.

Study Guide & Workbook – Chapter I

– Stop Wasting Your Life on Things You Can't Control

Summary

The chapter introduces the **"Let Them Theory"**, a mindset shift to reclaim personal power by releasing the need to control others' actions, opinions, or emotions. Key insights:

- **The Problem**: We often exhaust ourselves trying to manage others' perceptions or behaviors, believing it's the path to happiness (e.g., people-pleasing, over-explaining).

- **The Shift**: Focus on what *you* can control—your reactions, energy, and choices—while "letting" others be responsible for theirs.

- **The Catalyst**: The author's "prom story" illustrates how surrendering control ("Let them eat tacos in the rain!") reduced stress and improved relationships.

Key Takeaways

A. Core Lessons

- ☞ **You are not the problem**—giving away your power to others is.

- ♺ **"Let Them" is freedom**: Stop micromanaging others; focus on your own life.

- ☐ **Time is finite**: Struggling to control others wastes precious energy and joy.

B. The Let Them Theory in Action

Scenario	Old Response	"Let Them" Response
Critical parent	Defend your life choices	"Let them have their opinions."
Grumpy coworker	Take their mood personally	"Let them be in a bad mood."

Last-minute plans	Stress over others' disorganization	"Let them figure it out."

C. Why It Works

- **Science-backed**: Control is a psychological need, but overextending it creates stress.

- **Energy conservation**: Redirect effort from futile battles to meaningful actions.

Terminology

- **Let Them Theory**: Releasing the need to control others; accepting their autonomy.

- **Power Reclamation**: Shifting focus from external validation to internal agency.

- **Ice Cube Analogy**: Time melts away—prioritize what truly matters.

Real-World Applications

A. Personal Relationships

- *Example*: Instead of arguing with a partner over chores, say, "Let them load the dishwasher their way."

- *Outcome*: Fewer conflicts, more peace.

B. Workplace

- *Example*: A colleague takes credit for your idea. *Response*: "Let them have the spotlight; I'll document my contributions."

C. Social Media

- *Example*: Someone critiques your post. *Response*: "Let them disagree; my worth isn't tied to likes."

Interactive Workbook

I. Reflection Prompts

- **Your Turn**: *Write about a time you tried to control someone else's actions. How did it backfire?*

- **Journal**: *What's one relationship where "Let Them" could reduce tension?*

2. Analysis Exercises

- **Case Study**: Read the prom story again. *Underline moments where control escalated stress. How could "Let Them" have helped sooner?*

- **Compare/Contrast**: List 3 things you *can* vs. *can't* control in your life.

3. Application Tasks

- **Experiment**: For one day, practice saying "Let Them" in frustrating situations. *Record the results.*

- **Creative Project**: Design a "Let Them" reminder (e.g., phone wallpaper, sticky note).

Discussion Questions (Group/Book Club)

1. Why is surrendering control often harder than it seems?

2. How does societal pressure fuel our need to manage others?

3. Share an "aha!" moment from the chapter.

Professional Enhancements

Deep Dive (Optional)

- **Psychology**: Research "locus of control" and its impact on mental health.

- **Neuroscience**: How stress hormones respond to perceived lack of control.

Progress Tracker

- Practiced "Let Them" for 3 days.

- Identified one area to release control.

Next Steps

- **Read**: *The Subtle Art of Not Giving a Fck** (complementary themes).

- **Watch**: Author's TED Talk on emotional resilience.

Final Note: *"Let Them" isn't indifference—it's intentional focus on your own growth.*

Study Guide & Workbook – Chapter 2

– Getting Started: Let Them + Let Me

Summary

Chapter 2 expands the **Let Them Theory** by introducing **Let Me**—the critical second step that transforms passive detachment into empowered action. Key insights:

- **The Trigger**: The author's emotional spiral after seeing friends' vacation photos (feeling excluded) reveals how we internalize others' actions as personal rejection.

- **The Dual Framework**:

  - **Let Them**: Release control over others' choices (e.g., "Let them plan trips without me").

  - **Let Me**: Take responsibility for your response (e.g., "Let me rebuild neglected friendships").

- **The Danger of Half-Applying the Theory**: Using *only* "Let Them" can lead to isolation; pairing it with "Let Me" fosters growth and connection.

Key Takeaways

A. Core Lessons

- ☐ **"Let Them" ≠ Superiority**: It's not about judging others but freeing yourself from emotional weight.

- ⚲ **"Let Me" = Agency**: Shift focus to what *you* control—your actions, boundaries, and priorities.

- ⚔☐ **Balance Both Steps**: "Let Them" creates emotional space; "Let Me" fills it with intentional choices.

B. The Seesaw Analogy

Phase	Emotional State	Power Dynamic

Without "Let Them"	Heavy (insecure, jealous)	You feel "beneath" others
"Let Them"	Light (detached, superior)	You rise above the situation
"Let Me"	Empowered (accountable)	Balanced; focus on your agency

C. Psychological Roots

- **Stoicism**: Control only what's yours (your reactions).

- **Radical Acceptance**: Pain comes from resisting reality.

- **Detachment Theory**: Observe emotions without being consumed.

Terminology

- **Let Me Era**: Taking ownership of your happiness, goals, and relationships.

- **Power Reclamation**: Shifting energy from external control to internal action.

- **Illusion of Safety**: False belief that controlling others prevents pain.

Real-World Applications

A. Friendship Dynamics

- *Scenario*: Friends don't invite you to an event.
    - **Let Them**: "Let them have their plans."
    - **Let Me**: "Let me initiate the next gathering."

B. Workplace

- *Scenario*: A colleague dismisses your idea.
    - **Let Them**: "Let them overlook my contribution."
    - **Let Me**: "Let me advocate for myself in the next meeting."

C. Dating

- *Scenario*: Someone ghosts you.
    - **Let Them**: "Let them show their lack of interest."

    o   **Let Me**: "Let me invest in people who reciprocate."

Interactive Workbook

I. Reflection Prompts

- **Your Turn**: *Recall a time you felt excluded. How could "Let Them + Let Me" have changed your response?*

  Write Your Insights Here: ....

- **Journal**: *What's one area of life where you default to control? What's one "Let Me" action you can take?*

2. Analysis Exercises

- **Case Study**: Re-read the "girls' trip" story. *Underline moments where the author shifts from blame ("Why wasn't I invited?") to accountability ("I haven't invested in these friendships").*

- **Compare/Contrast**: List 3 things you've tried to control in others vs. 3 things you *can* control in yourself.

3. Application Tasks

- **Experiment**: For one week, practice "Let Them + Let Me" when feeling slighted. *Example:*

      o   **Trigger**: Partner leaves dishes in the sink.

      o   **Let Them**: "Let them clean (or not) on their timeline."

      o   **Let Me**: "Let me communicate my needs calmly."

- **Creative Project**: Design a "Let Me Manifesto" (e.g., "Let Me prioritize joy over perfection").

Discussion Questions (Group/Book Club)

1. Why is "Let Me" harder than "Let Them"? How does society discourage personal accountability?

2. Share an example where "superiority" masked a deeper need for connection.

3. How can "Let Me" prevent loneliness when applying the theory?

Professional Enhancements

Deep Dive (Optional)

- **Neuroscience**: How the brain's amygdala triggers control impulses under stress.

- **Attachment Theory**: How early relationships shape our need to manage others.

Progress Tracker

- Practiced "Let Them + Let Me" for 3+ days.

- Identified one "control habit" to release.

Next Steps

- **Read**: *The Gifts of Imperfection* (Brené Brown) on worthiness vs. control.

- **Watch**: TED Talk on "The Power of Vulnerability."

Final Note: *"Let Them" is the pause; "Let Me" is the play. Master both to rewrite your life's script.*

Study Guide & Workbook – Chapter 3

– Shocker: Life Is Stressful

Summary

Chapter 3 applies the **Let Them Theory** to **stress management**, revealing how small daily irritations hijack our emotional state—and how to reclaim control. Key insights:

- **The Stress Epidemic**: Chronic stress locks us in "fight or flight" mode (amygdala dominance), impairing decision-making and happiness.

- **The Let Them Reset**:

    o **Let Them**: Detach from uncontrollable stressors (e.g., slow cashiers, traffic).

    o **Let Me**: Take actionable steps to protect your peace (e.g., deep breathing, setting boundaries).

- **Neuroscience Backing**: Harvard's Dr. Aditi Nerurkar explains how stress physiologically hijacks the brain—and how "Let Them" acts as an "off switch."

Key Takeaways

A. Core Lessons

- ☐ **Brain Science**: Stress shifts control from the logical **prefrontal cortex** to the reactive **amygdala** (survival mode).

- ⟳ **Dual Response**:

    o *Let Them*: "Let the coughing passenger be." (Release control)

    o *Let Me*: "Let me wear headphones and a scarf." (Take action)

- ⚡ **Power Paradox**: Trying to control others drains energy; focusing on your response multiplies it.

B. The Airport Stress Test

Stress Trigger	Old Reaction	"Let Them + Let Me" Response
Flight delay	Fume at gate agents	"Let them manage logistics. Let me read a book."
Rude passenger	Complain loudly	"Let them be rude. Let me move seats."
Lost luggage	Blame airline	"Let them locate it. Let me buy essentials."

C. Stress Hacks from Dr. Aditi

1. **Pause:** Say "Let Them" to disengage the amygdala.

2. **Breathe:** "Let Me take 3 deep breaths" to activate the vagus nerve (calming signal).

3. **Refocus:** Shift attention to what you *can* control.

Terminology

- **Amygdala Hijack:** When stress triggers impulsive, emotional reactions.

- **Vagus Nerve Reset:** Deep breathing to exit fight-or-flight mode.

- **Death by 1,000 Cuts:** Accumulated stress from minor irritations.

Real-World Applications

A. Daily Annoyances

- *Scenario:* Slow walkers blocking your path.
    - **Let Them:** "Let them stroll at their pace."
    - **Let Me:** "Let me step around them calmly."

B. Workplace

- *Scenario:* Micromanaging boss.
    - **Let Them:** "Let them request unnecessary updates."
    - **Let Me:** "Let me proactively share progress reports."

C. Relationships

- *Scenario:* Partner leaves dishes undone.

- o **Let Them:** "Let them clean (or not) on their timeline."

- o **Let Me:** "Let me communicate needs without nagging."

Interactive Workbook

1. Reflection Prompts

- **Your Turn:** *What's one "small stressor" that disproportionately irritates you? How could "Let Them + Let Me" help?*

  Write Your Insights Here: ....

- **Journal:** *Track your stress triggers for 3 days. Which were controllable vs. uncontrollable?*

2. Analysis Exercises

- **Case Study:** Re-read the "coughing passenger" story. *Highlight where the author shifts from frustration to empowered action.*

- **Compare/Contrast:** List 3 stressors you've tried to control vs. 3 *effective* responses you've used.

3. Application Tasks

- **Experiment:** Use the "Let Them + Let Me" method for minor stressors this week. *Example:*

  - o **Trigger:** Long grocery line.

  - o **Let Them:** "Let the cashier take their time."

  - o **Let Me:** "Let me listen to a podcast while I wait."

- **Creative Project:** Design a "Stress Reset Card" for your wallet with prompts:

  - o *"Let Them: _____."*

  - o *"Let Me: _____."*

Discussion Questions (Group/Book Club)

1. Why do we often *prefer* blaming others over taking responsibility for our reactions?

2. Share a time when reframing stress ("Let Them") improved your day.

3. How can workplaces apply "Let Them + Let Me" to reduce burnout?

Professional Enhancements

Deep Dive (Optional)

- **Neuroplasticity**: How consistent "Let Them" practice rewires the brain's stress response.

- **Cultural Stressors**: Societal pressures that amplify control tendencies (e.g., "hustle culture").

Progress Tracker

- Used "Let Them + Let Me" for 5+ stressors.

- Identified one automatic stress reaction to reprogram.

Next Steps

- **Read**: *Why Zebras Don't Get Ulcers* (Robert Sapolsky) on stress biology.

- **Watch**: TED Talk on "How to Make Stress Your Friend."

Final Note: *"Let Them" is the pause button; "Let Me" is the play button. Master both to direct your life's movie.*

Study Guide & Workbook – Chapter 4

– Let Them Stress You Out

Applying the "Let Them Theory" to Manage Workplace and Life Stress

---

Summary

This chapter explores how to apply the **"Let Them Theory"**—accepting what you cannot control ("Let Them") while taking ownership of your response ("Let Me")—to reduce stress, particularly in work environments. Key themes include:

- Workplace stress is inevitable, but your reaction determines its impact.

- You cannot control others (e.g., bosses, coworkers, policies), but you **can** control your career choices.

- Chronic stress leads to burnout; shifting focus to actionable solutions ("Let Me") empowers you.

Key Takeaways

1. The Problem: External Stressors Are Inevitable

- Work is a major stressor (e.g., unfair promotions, micromanagement, layoffs).

- Others' actions (e.g., a boss delaying a promotion) trigger frustration, but **you choose how long to endure it.**

2. The Truth: Stress Responses Are Automatic, But Manageable

- Emotional reactions (anger, powerlessness) are natural but can be reset.

- Fixating on uncontrollable factors wastes energy and clouds judgment.

3. The Solution: "Let Them" + "Let Me" Framework

Let Them	Let Me
Accept others' actions (e.g., "Let my boss delay my promotion").	Take responsibility for your response (e.g., "Let me update my resume").

Stop trying to change what you can't control.	Redirect energy toward actions within your power.

Real-World Applications

- **Career Growth**: Instead of waiting for a promotion, seek new opportunities.

- **Daily Stressors**: Use the "1-Hour Rule"—if an issue won't matter in an hour, let it go.

- **Politics/Social Issues**: Engage constructively (e.g., advocacy) or disengage to protect mental health.

Terminology

- **Let Them Theory**: A mindset dividing situations into "uncontrollable" (accept) and "actionable" (own).

- **Amygdala Hijack**: The brain's stress response triggering impulsive reactions; the theory helps reset it.

- **Chronic Stress**: Persistent stress leading to burnout; countered by proactive "Let Me" steps.

Interactive Workbook

Reflection Prompts

1. *"What's one work stressor I've been trying to control? How can I 'Let Them' and shift to 'Let Me'?" (Write Your Insights Here:)*

2. *"Recall a time when stress clouded your judgment. How could the '1-Hour Rule' have helped?"*

Analysis Exercise

Case Study: A coworker takes credit for your idea.

- **Let Them**: "They'll always seek recognition."

- **Let Me**: "I'll document contributions and discuss credit with my manager."

Application Task

- **Action Plan**: List 3 stressors. For each, write one "Let Them" and one "Let Me" response.

Stressor	Let Them	Let Me
Boss ignores emails	"They're overwhelmed."	"I'll follow up in person."

Discussion Questions (Group/Book Club)

1. How does societal pressure (e.g., "hustle culture") conflict with the "Let Them Theory"?

2. Can "Let Them" ever feel like giving up? How do you balance acceptance with accountability?

Professional Enhancements

Deep Dive: Bloom's Taxonomy in Action

- **Remember**: Define "Let Them Theory."

- **Apply**: Role-play a stressor using the framework.

- **Evaluate**: Debate: "Is disengaging from politics a valid 'Let Me' strategy?"

Progress Tracker

- Completed reflection prompts.

- Practiced "Let Them" in one real-life situation.

- Researched one new job opportunity ("Let Me").

Next Steps

- **Read**: *"The Subtle Art of Not Giving a F*ck"** by Mark Manson (complementary mindset).

- **Try**: A "Let Them" journal for one week—note stressors and your responses.

Final Thought: *"You can't control the wind, but you can adjust your sails."* Use this chapter to navigate stress with agency, not frustration.

Study Guide & Workbook – Chapter 5

– Let Them Think Bad Thoughts About You

Freeing Yourself from the Fear of Judgment

Summary

This chapter dismantles the paralyzing fear of others' opinions using the **"Let Them Theory"**:

- **Core Problem**: We self-censor, procrastinate, and avoid risks due to imagined judgments.

- **Liberating Truth**: You *cannot* control others' thoughts—but you *can* control your response.

- **Framework**:

  o **Let Them**: Allow others to think what they want (e.g., "Let them call me arrogant for posting my achievements").

  o **Let Me**: Prioritize actions aligned with *your* values (e.g., "Let me share my work boldly").

Key Takeaways

1. The Cost of Caring Too Much

- Fear of judgment leads to:

  o Procrastination ("I'll fail, so I won't start").

  o Perfectionism ("It must be flawless or I'll be mocked").

  o Self-rejection (Editing yourself before others can).

- *Example*: The author delayed marketing her speaking business for **2 years** to avoid friends' opinions.

2. The Science of Letting Go

- **Neurological Fact**: Humans have ~70,000 daily thoughts—most are uncontrollable.

- **Paradox**: Even loved ones think negative thoughts about you (*and vice versa*). It's normal.

3. The "Let Them" Mindset

Fear-Based Response	"Let Them" Response
"What if they think I'm selfish for quitting my job?"	"Let them think that. I'm choosing my health."
"I can't post this—it's not good enough."	"Let them scroll past. I'm sharing my progress."

Real-World Applications

- **Career**: Post about your business (*even if it feels "braggy"*).

- **Relationships**: Make decisions that make *you* proud (e.g., visiting grandparents *for you*, not guilt).

- **Self-Expression**: Wear, create, or speak as *you* want—not as others expect.

Terminology

- **Self-Rejection**: Preemptively dimming your light to avoid others' criticism.

- **Amygdala Hijack**: Stress response triggered by perceived judgment; "Let Them" resets it.

- **Values-Driven Decisions**: Choosing actions based on *your* priorities, not external approval.

Interactive Workbook

Reflection Prompts

1. *"What's one thing I've avoided due to fear of judgment? How would 'Let Them' change this?"*

   (Write Your Insights Here:)

---

2. *"Recall a time you edited yourself. What did it cost you?"*

Analysis Exercise

Case Study: A friend scoffs at your dream to start a podcast.

- **Fear-Based**: "Maybe it's a dumb idea."

- **Let Them**: "Let them doubt. I'll record Episode 1 anyway."

Application Task

- **"Let Me" Challenge**: Do *one* thing you've avoided due to judgment (e.g., post art, speak up in a meeting).

- **Journal**: How did it feel? What surprised you?

Discussion Questions (Group/Book Club)

1. *"Why is 'just stop caring' unhelpful advice? How does 'Let Them' reframe it?"*

2. *"Can you think of a historical figure who succeeded because they embraced 'Let Them'?"*

Professional Enhancements

Deep Dive: Bloom's Taxonomy in Action

- **Analyze**: Compare societal messages (e.g., "Be humble") vs. "Let Them."

- **Create**: Design a "Let Them" mantra for your biggest fear.

Progress Tracker

- Completed one "Let Me" action.

- Identified a recurring self-rejection pattern.

- Shared a "Let Them" win with a friend.

Next Steps

- **Read**: *"The Gifts of Imperfection"* by Brené Brown (on worthiness).

- **Try**: A "Judgment Detox" week—track how often you assume others' opinions.

Final Thought: *"Your life shrinks or expands in proportion to your courage."*—Anaïs Nin. Use "Let Them" to expand.

Study Guide & Workbook – Chapter 6

– How to Love Difficult People

Applying the Let Them Theory to Family Dynamics

Summary

This chapter explores how to use the **Let Them Theory** with family—the most challenging relationships to navigate due to deep emotional ties and lifelong expectations. Key themes include:

- **Family Dynamics**: Loved ones often express opinions bluntly because they feel invested in your happiness.

- **Frame of Reference**: Understanding *why* family members think the way they do (based on their life experiences) fosters compassion.

- **Boundaries with Love**: "Let Them" have their opinions; "Let Me" choose how to respond in alignment with *your* values.

Key Takeaways

1. Why Family Hits Different

- **Proximity**: Unlike coworkers or friends, family is "with you for life"—opinions feel more personal.

- **Bluntness**: They voice disapproval openly (e.g., "You're ruining your life by dropping out of school").

- **Systems Theory**: Families operate as interconnected webs; any change (e.g., divorce, career shifts) sends shockwaves.

2. The Frame of Reference Tool

- **Definition**: The lens through which someone interprets a situation, shaped by their past.

    - *Example*: The author's mom resisted her marriage because *her own* experience involved moving far from family.

- **Power**: Recognizing a loved one's Frame of Reference reduces conflict (e.g., "They're not rejecting me—they're scared").

3. Navigating Control vs. Care

Control	Care
"You *must* come home for the holidays."	"I miss you and want to spend time together."
"Your career choice is a mistake."	"I worry this path will be hard for you."

4. Step parenting & Blended Families

- **Let Them**: Allow stepchildren to grieve the family they lost.

- **Let Me**: Be the compassionate adult who creates space for new bonds to form.

Terminology

- **Family System**: The interdependent relationships and unspoken rules in a family unit.

- **Projection**: When family members impose *their* unmet needs/regrets onto your choices.

- **Values-Driven Boundaries**: Limits set based on *your* needs (e.g., "I'll visit, but I won't discuss my divorce").

Interactive Workbook

Reflection Prompts

1. *"Think of a family opinion that stung. What might their 'Frame of Reference' be?"*
   (Write Your Insights Here:)

---

2. *"What's one family expectation you've outgrown? How can 'Let Them' free you?"*

Analysis Exercise

Case Study: Your sibling says you're "selfish" for moving abroad.

- **Their Frame of Reference**: Fear of losing closeness (e.g., past abandonment).

- **Let Them**: "Let them feel upset. It's not about me."

- **Let Me**: "I'll schedule regular calls to stay connected."

Application Tasks

- **"Frame of Reference" Journal**: Interview a family member about a past decision *they* made. Note how it shapes their views today.

- **Boundary Script**: Draft a response to a recurring criticism (e.g., "I hear your concern, but this is my choice").

Discussion Questions (Group/Book Club)

1. *"Can you think of a family conflict that improved with understanding their 'Frame of Reference'?"*

2. *"How do cultural traditions complicate 'Let Them' with family?"*

Professional Enhancements

Deep Dive: Bloom's Taxonomy in Action

- **Analyze**: Compare two generations' Frames of Reference (e.g., "Why does Grandma equate divorce with failure?").

- **Create**: Design a "Family Values Charter" outlining how disagreements will be handled.

Progress Tracker

- Practiced "Let Them" during one family tension.

- Identified one inherited belief to reevaluate.

- Shared a "Frame of Reference" insight with a loved one.

Next Steps

- **Read**: *"Adult Children of Emotionally Immature Parents"* by Lindsay Gibson (for deeper healing).

- **Try**: A "No Guilt" experiment—decline one family request without apologizing.

Final Thought: *"Family isn't about perfection. It's about showing up—for them, and for yourself."*

Study Guide & Workbook – Chapter 7

– When Grown-Ups Throw Tantrums

Managing Emotional Immaturity in Relationships

Summary

This chapter reveals how adults often display childlike emotional behaviors and teaches how to use the **Let Them Theory** to:

- **Stop managing others' emotions**: Recognize you're not responsible for another adult's reactions.

- **Set boundaries**: Respond to tantrums, silent treatments, and guilt trips with compassion—without caving.

- **Regulate your own emotions**: Learn to let feelings rise and pass without impulsive reactions.

Key insight: *"Most adults are just eight-year-olds in bigger bodies when it comes to emotional maturity."*

Key Takeaways

1. The Problem: Emotional Immaturity is Everywhere

- **Common adult behaviors** mirror childhood patterns:

Child Behavior	Adult Equivalent
Sulking in a corner	Silent treatment
Throwing tantrums	Rage-texting/outbursts
Lying to avoid trouble	White lies or denial

- **Impact on you**: These behaviors drain your energy and manipulate your decisions (e.g., saying "yes" to avoid guilt).

2. The Science of Emotions

- **90-Second Rule**: Emotions are chemical bursts that dissipate in ~90 seconds if you don't react.

- **Contagion:** Emotions spread (e.g., someone's bad mood triggers yours).

- **Triggers:** Hunger, stress, or exhaustion amplify emotional reactions.

3. The Solution: "Let Them" + "Let Me" Framework

- **Let Them:** Allow others to have their emotional outbursts without fixing or fearing them.

  - *Example:* "Let my mom sulk when I set a boundary."

- **Let Me:** Choose how *you* respond (e.g., "Let me stay calm and walk away").

4. Applying the Theory to Yourself

- **When *you're* the emotional one:**

  - Pause before reacting (don't text, vent, or numb the feeling).

  - Ask: *"Would I tolerate this behavior from an 8-year-old?"*

Terminology

- **Emotional Immaturity:** Inability to process feelings constructively (e.g., silent treatment, blame-shifting).

- **Boundary:** A limit set to protect your energy (e.g., "I won't engage when you yell").

- **Emotional Contagion:** The phenomenon where one person's emotions trigger similar feelings in others.

Interactive Workbook

Reflection Prompts

1. *"Who in my life acts like an '8-year-old' during conflict? How do I usually respond?"*
   (Write Your Insights Here:)

---

2. *"Recall a time you reacted immaturely. What triggered it?"*

Analysis Exercise

Case Study: Your partner gives you the silent treatment after a disagreement.

- **Childlike Behavior**: Sulking instead of communicating.

- **Let Them**: "Let them process their emotions."

- **Let Me**: "I'll give space but won't chase or apologize for setting a boundary."

Application Tasks

- **90-Second Experiment**: Next time you're upset, pause for 90 seconds before reacting. Journal the result.

- **Boundary Script**: Draft a response to a frequent guilt-trip (e.g., *"I understand you're upset, but I won't change my decision."*).

Discussion Questions (Group/Book Club)

1. *"Why do you think society tolerates adult tantrums more than child tantrums?"*

2. *"How can 'Let Them' backfire if used without compassion?"*

Professional Enhancements

Deep Dive: Bloom's Taxonomy in Action

- **Analyze**: Compare a recent conflict to the child/adult behavior chart.

- **Create**: Design a "Trigger Toolkit" (e.g., calming phrases, exit strategies) for heated moments.

Progress Tracker

- Practiced the 90-second pause once.

- Identified one relationship where I need firmer boundaries.

- Used "Let Them" during someone's outburst.

Next Steps

- **Read**: *"Adult Children of Emotionally Immature Parents"* by Lindsay Gibson (for deeper patterns).

- **Try**: A "No Fixing" week—don't manage anyone else's emotions.

Final Thought: *"You aren't required to set yourself on fire to keep others warm."*

Study Guide & Workbook – Chapter 8

– The Right Decision Often Feels Wrong

Navigating Difficult Choices Despite Emotional Resistance

Summary

This chapter tackles the paradox that **the right decisions often feel emotionally wrong** when they disappoint others. Through the lens of a groom questioning his wedding, we learn:

- **Core Dilemma:** Logic says one thing (call off the wedding), but emotions scream another (fear of hurting people).

- **Emotional Truth:** Pain is inevitable when making tough choices—but avoiding it creates *longer-term suffering*.

- **Framework:**

  o **Let Them:** Allow others to feel upset, angry, or disappointed.

  o **Let Me:** Choose what aligns with *your* truth, even when it's heartbreaking.

Key quote: *"Easier now makes it way harder later."*

Key Takeaways

1. Why Right Decisions Feel Wrong

- **Emotional Hijacking:** Fear of others' reactions (e.g., anger, guilt) overrides logic.

- **Avoidance Cycle:** We stay in wrong jobs/relationships to dodge short-term pain.

- **Healthy Agony:** Doubting a big decision is *normal*—it shows you care.

2. The "Emotional Wave" Analogy

- Emotions rise and fall like ocean waves. Even hurricanes (e.g., calling off a wedding) pass.

- *Example:* Parents may rage about lost deposits—but eventually, they'll understand.

3. The Let Them Theory in Action

Situation	Let Them	Let Me
Calling off an engagement	"Let them be heartbroken."	"Let me choose honesty over a lifetime of regret."
Quitting a stable job	"Let them call me reckless."	"Let me prioritize my mental health."

Real-World Applications

- **Relationships**: End things *before* resentment builds.

- **Career**: Leave unfulfilling work, even if it disappoints your family.

- **Self-Honesty**: Speak up when you've been wronged (e.g., confront a dishonest friend).

Terminology

- **Emotional Responsibility**: Recognizing you're *not* accountable for others' feelings.

- **Avoidance Tax**: The compounding cost of delaying hard choices (e.g., wasted years in a dead-end job).

- **Values-Aligned Decision**: A choice that honors *your* needs, not others' expectations.

Interactive Workbook

Reflection Prompts

1. *"What's one decision I've avoided due to fear of reactions? What's it costing me?"*
   (Write Your Insights Here:)

---

2. *"Recall a time you made a hard but right choice. How did the 'emotional wave' play out?"*

Analysis Exercise

Case Study: You're offered a dream job abroad, but your family begs you to stay.

- **Let Them**: "Let them fear losing me."

- **Let Me**: "Let me pursue growth—I can visit often."

Application Tasks

- **"Wave-Riding" Practice**: Next time you're anxious about a decision, set a 24-hour timer. Observe how emotions shift.

- **Script Draft**: Write a tough conversation you've avoided (e.g., *"I love you, but this relationship isn't working."*).

Discussion Questions (Group/Book Club)

1. *"Why do society/family often equate 'hard decisions' with 'selfishness'?"*

2. *"How can we support others through their hard choices without guilt-tripping?"*

Professional Enhancements

Deep Dive: Bloom's Taxonomy in Action

- **Evaluate**: Compare societal messages (e.g., "Don't quit!") vs. psychological research on regret.

- **Create**: Design a "Decision-Making Compass" with your core values.

Progress Tracker

- Identified one avoided decision.

- Practiced "wave-riding" with a small choice (e.g., saying no to a request).

- Shared a hard decision story with a trusted friend.

Next Steps

- **Read**: *"The Top Five Regrets of the Dying"* by Bronnie Ware (on courage vs. conformity).

- **Try**: A "No Guilt" experiment—make one values-aligned choice without apologizing.

Final Thought: *"Your future self will thank you for the hard choices you make today."*

Study Guide & Workbook – Chapter 9

– Yes, Life Isn't Fair

Mastering Self-Comparison & Turning Adversity into Advantage

Summary

This chapter confronts the universal struggle of comparing ourselves to others and the paralyzing effects of believing life "should" be fair. The author argues that **comparison becomes toxic when we fixate on unchangeable circumstances** (e.g., genetics, luck, others' privileges) but can be transformative if used as a **teacher** rather than **torture**. Key metaphors include:

- **"The Card Game of Life"**: You can't control the hand you're dealt, only how you play it.

- **"Torture vs. Teacher"**: Two types of comparison—one drains power, the other fuels growth.

Key Takeaways

I. Life Is Inherently Unfair

- Everyone faces unequal starting points (genetics, wealth, health, opportunities).

- **Fixating on fairness wastes energy**; acceptance frees you to act.

2. Comparison: Torture vs. Teacher

Torture (Harmful)	Teacher (Helpful)
Obsessing over unchangeable traits (e.g., height, family wealth).	Learning from others' strategies, habits, or mindsets.
Upward comparison ("They're better than me").	Downward comparison ("I have privileges others don't").

Leads to shame, procrastination, self-hatred.	Sparks motivation, adaptability, gratitude.

3. Focus on Agency

- **Control what you can**: Your effort, mindset, and reactions.

- **Let go of what you can't**: Others' advantages or luck.

4. Real-World Consequences

- Chronic comparison links to mental health struggles (eating disorders, addiction, low self-esteem).

- **Solution**: Redirect focus to *your* game—not others'.

Terminology

- **Upward Comparison**: Measuring yourself against those you perceive as "better."

- **Downward Comparison**: Contrasting your situation with those less fortunate (builds gratitude).

- **Fixed vs. Malleable Traits**: Fixed = unchangeable (e.g., birthplace); malleable = improvable (e.g., skills).

Real-World Applications

I. Social Media Audit

- Unfollow accounts that trigger "torture" comparisons.

- Follow accounts that *teach* (e.g., skill-building, resilience stories).

2. The "30-Second Test"

When envious, ask: *"Can I change this in 30 seconds?"* If no, label it "fixed" and move on.

3. Gratitude Counterbalance

List 3 privileges you have (e.g., clean water, education) when feeling "behind."

Interactive Workbook

Reflection Prompts

1. **"My Comparison Triggers"**:

   o *What situations or people make me feel inadequate? Why?*

   o *Your Turn:* Write your insights here:

   _____

2. **Fixed vs. Malleable Inventory**

   o List 3 "fixed" traits you resent in others. Now, list 3 *malleable* traits you admire and could develop.

Analysis Exercise

Case Study: Sawyer vs. Kendall

- *How does Sawyer's fixation on Kendall's "fixed" traits harm her?*

- *What could Sawyer gain by shifting to "teacher" comparisons?*

Application Tasks

1. "Play Your Hand" Journal

- Describe one "unfair" card you've been dealt. Brainstorm 3 ways to *play it better.*

2. 24-Hour No-Comparison Challenge

- Avoid all comparisons for a day. Note how it affects your mood/productivity.

Discussion Questions (Group/Book Club)

1. *"Is it possible to eliminate comparison entirely? Why or why not?"*

2. *How can society's emphasis on "fairness" both help and hinder growth?*

Deep Dive (Optional)

Research Spotlight: Studies show upward comparison lowers self-esteem, while downward comparison boosts life satisfaction (*Social Psychology Quarterly*, 2021).

Progress Tracker

- Completed reflection prompts.
- Tried the 30-Second Test for 3 days.
- Shared one insight with a friend.

Next Steps

- **Read**: *The Gap and The Gain* by Dan Sullivan (focuses on self-measurement).
- **Practice**: Weekly "gratitude vs. envy" journaling.

Final Thought: *"The game isn't about holding the best cards—it's about playing yours with courage and creativity."*

Study Guide & Workbook – Chapter 10

– How to Make Comparison Your Teacher

Transforming Jealousy into Fuel for Growth

Summary

This chapter reframes **comparison as a strategic tool** rather than a source of suffering. Building on Chapter 9's "torture vs. teacher" framework, the author argues that envy reveals unmet ambitions and provides a **blueprint for action**. Key metaphors include:

- **"Jealousy as an Invitation"**: A signal from your future self about what you truly desire.

- **"Putting in the Reps"**: Success comes from consistent, mundane effort (like gym workouts).

Key Takeaways

1. The Two Faces of Comparison

Torture (Ch. 9)	Teacher (Ch. 10)
Focuses on *fixed* traits (genetics, luck).	Highlights *malleable* achievements (skills, habits).
Drains motivation; fosters victimhood.	Provides a roadmap for growth.
Example: "They're naturally talented."	Example: "They built a business—I can learn their steps."

2. Jealousy = Data

- **Ask**: *"What does this envy reveal about my unmet goals?"* (e.g., Molly's irritation exposed her procrastination on social media).

- **Flip the script**: "If they can do it, so can I."

3. The "Let Them" Mindset

- **Let Them** succeed → **Let Them** inspire you → **Let Me** act.

- Case Study: The author's jealousy of a friend's dream home forced her to confront her own financial passivity.

4. Success Requires "Reps"

- **Tom Brady's Formula**: Consistency > "specialness."

- **Actionable Truth**: 95% of goals are achievable through discipline, not luck.

Terminology

- **"Putting in the Reps"**: Daily, incremental effort toward a goal.

- **Upward Comparison (Teacher Mode)**: Studying others' *processes* (not just outcomes).

- **Let Them Theory**: Allowing others' success to *guide* (not diminish) you.

Real-World Applications

1. The "Inspiration Audit"

- Identify 3 people who trigger jealousy. List *specific, learnable* strategies they use.

2. Anger-to-Action Protocol

1. **Name the envy** (e.g., "I'm mad about X's promotion").

2. **Ask**: *"What work did they put in that I've avoided?"*

3. **Commit to one "rep"** (e.g., "Today, I'll update my resume").

3. Social Media Reboot

- Replace "torture" accounts with "teacher" accounts (e.g., follow creators who share *how* they succeeded).

Interactive Workbook

Reflection Prompts

1. **"My Jealousy Journal"**

    o *Think of a recent envy spike. What did it teach you about your desires?*

    o **Your Turn:**_____

2. **Fixed vs. Learnable Inventory**

    o List 3 traits you envy in others. Label each *fixed* ($\not\!\!\!\!$) or *learnable* (📚).

Analysis Exercise

Case Study: Molly's Meltdown

1. How did Molly's jealousy *distract* her vs. *guide* her?

2. What "reps" had her rival put in that Molly avoided?

Application Tasks

I. "Steal Their Homework"

- Choose someone you admire. Reverse-engineer *one* habit/system they use.

2. 7-Day Rep Challenge

- Pick a goal. Do *one small action* daily (e.g., "Post I LinkedIn update").

Discussion Questions (Group/Book Club)

1. *"Is anger a valid motivator? When does it help or backfire?"*

2. *How can society's "overnight success" narratives hinder growth?*

Deep Dive (Optional)

Research Spotlight:

- Studies show **proactive envy** (using jealousy as fuel) increases performance (*Journal of Personality and Social Psychology*, 2020).

Progress Tracker

- Completed "Inspiration Audit."

- Logged 7 "reps" this week.

- Shared one lesson from jealousy with a friend.

Next Steps

- **Read**: *Atomic Habits* by James Clear (mastering consistency).

- **Practice**: Weekly "reverse-engineering" of a role model's success.

Final Thought: *"Comparison isn't the thief of joy—it's the compass. The real theft is ignoring its directions."*

Study Guide & Workbook – Chapter 11

– The Truth No One Told You About Adult Friendship

Navigating the Shifting Landscape of Connection

Summary

This chapter dissects why adult friendships feel harder than childhood bonds and introduces **three pillars** (proximity, timing, energy) that sustain them. The author reframes friendship loss as a natural result of *The Great Scattering*—the post-20s divergence of life paths—and offers the **Let Them Theory** to release control and cultivate flexibility.

Key Metaphors:

- **"Friendship as a Group Sport → Solo Activity"**: Childhood's structured togetherness vs. adulthood's intentional effort.

- **"Seasons of Friendship"**: Some bonds last a lifetime; others fade naturally.

Key Takeaways

1. The Great Scattering

- **What Changes**: After age 20, shared routines (school, milestones) vanish. Friends disperse geographically and emotionally.

- **Why It Hurts**: We expect childhood's passive closeness but face adulthood's active maintenance.

- **Let Them Mindset**: *"Let Them move away. Let Them prioritize new friends. Let Them not text me."*

2. Three Pillars of Adult Friendship

Pillar	Definition	Example
Proximity	Physical nearness; requires ~200 hours for closeness.	Coworkers you see daily vs. long-distance friends.

Timing	Alignment in life stages (career, parenthood, etc.).	New parents bonding over sleepless nights.
Energy	Natural "click"—or lack thereof— between people.	College roommates who outgrow each other.

3. Let Them Theory in Action

- **Release Expectations**: Friendships ebb and flow; forcing them drains energy.

- **Proactive Steps**: Seek proximity (join clubs), honor timing (find peers in similar phases), trust energy (let go of forced bonds).

Terminology

- **The Great Scattering**: Post-20s fragmentation of friend groups due to diverging life paths.

- **"Best Friend" Fallacy**: Labeling creates unrealistic pressure; friendships evolve.

- **Let Them Theory**: Accepting others' choices without taking them personally.

Real-World Applications

1. Proximity Hack

- **Action**: Attend one recurring local event (e.g., book club, gym class) to accumulate "friendship hours."

- **Research Backing**: University of Kansas study shows 50+ hours create casual bonds; 200+ for closeness.

2. Timing Audit

- **Reflect**: *"Which friendships feel strained due to mismatched life stages? How can I adjust expectations?"*

3. Energy Check

- **Signs to Let Go**: Conversations feel forced; you dread interactions.

- **Signs to Invest**: Conversations flow; you feel energized afterward.

Interactive Workbook

Reflection Prompts

1. **"My Great Scattering"**

   o *List 3 friendships that faded due to proximity/timing. What did you learn?*

   o **Your Turn:**_____

2. **Pillar Assessment**

   o Rank your top 3 current friendships by pillar strength (e.g., "Sarah: Proximity 8/10, Timing 5/10, Energy 9/10").

Analysis Exercise

Case Study: Workplace Loneliness

- *Why might someone spend 40+ hours/week with coworkers but still feel friendless?*

- *How could the "Three Pillars" explain this?*

Application Tasks

1. "Intentional Reconnection"

- Pick one long-distance friend. Schedule a quarterly video call with a shared activity (e.g., watching the same movie).

2. "Energy Experiment"

- For one week, note which friendships leave you energized/drained. Adjust time invested accordingly.

Discussion Questions (Group/Book Club)

1. *"Is the 'best friend' label harmful or helpful in adulthood?"*

2. *How can social media distort our perception of others' friendships?*

Deep Dive (Optional)

Research Spotlight:

- A 2022 *Journal of Social and Personal Relationships* study found **proximity** matters more than similarity in forming adult bonds.

Progress Tracker

- Completed "Pillar Assessment" for 3 friends.

- Scheduled one intentional reconnection.

- Shared a friendship insight with a group.

Next Steps

- **Read:** *Platonic* by Marisa G. Franco (science of making adult friends).

- **Practice:** Monthly "friendship audit" using the Three Pillars.

Final Thought: *"Adult friendship isn't about recapturing childhood's ease—it's about crafting deeper bonds with intention."*

Study Guide & Workbook – Chapter 12

– Why Some Friendships Naturally Fade

Understanding the Organic Evolution of Relationships

Summary

This chapter explores the **natural lifecycle of friendships** through a personal story about shifting social dynamics in adulthood. The author reveals how **proximity, timing, and energy** (the Three Pillars from Chapter 11) influence bonds—and why clinging to outdated expectations creates suffering. Key insights:

- **Friendship fade ≠ failure**: It's often a neutral result of changing circumstances.

- **The "Let Them" mindset**: Releasing control over others' choices preserves self-respect and emotional energy.

- **Case Study**: The author's jealousy when her close-knit mom group evolved without her, and how she mishandled it.

Key Metaphor:

- **"Friendship Seasons"**: Like nature, relationships have cycles of growth, dormancy, and renewal.

Key Takeaways

I. Why Friendships Fade

Cause	Example	"Let Them" Response
Proximity Shift	Friends move neighborhoods/jobs.	*"Let Them build local connections."*
Timing Mismatch	One friend becomes a parent; the other stays single.	*"Let Them prioritize their current chapter."*
Energy Change	Conversations feel forced or draining.	*"Let Them drift if the connection fades."*

2. Toxic vs. Healthy Responses

- **Toxic**: Blaming others, keeping score, forcing interactions.

- **Healthy**: Assuming good intent, celebrating others' joy, investing where energy is reciprocated.

3. The Reconnection Paradox

- Friendships can **reactivate** when pillars realign (e.g., old friends reuniting after kids leave home).

- **Action Step**: Send the "nostalgia text" (*"Remember when we...? Miss you!"*).

Terminology

- **"Friendship Red Flag"**: Behaviors that strain bonds (e.g., jealousy, scorekeeping).

- **Nostalgia Text**: A low-pressure message to rekindle dormant friendships.

- **One-Sided Effort**: When one person consistently initiates contact (a sign to reassess).

Real-World Applications

1. The "Pillar Check"

- Every 6 months, assess key friendships: *Has proximity/timing/energy shifted?* Adjust expectations accordingly.

2. Jealousy Journaling

- When envy arises, write: *"What does this reveal about my unmet needs?"* (e.g., the author's need for belonging).

3. The 2-Touch Rule

- Reach out twice; if no response, *Let Them* go without drama. Revisit in 6 months.

Interactive Workbook

Reflection Prompts

1. **"My Faded Friendship"**

   o *Recall a friendship that faded. Which pillar (proximity/timing/energy) shifted?*

   o **Your Turn:**_____

2. **Scorekeeping Audit**

   o *Do you mentally track who texts first? How does this affect your joy?*

Analysis Exercise

Case Study: The Suburban Mom Group

1. How did proximity accelerate the author's friends' bond?

2. What could she have done differently using the *Let Them Theory*?

Application Tasks

1. **"Nostalgia Text Challenge"**

   • Contact one "dormant" friend with a warm, no-pressure message.

2. **"Energy Map"**

   • Chart your 5 closest friends. Note who energizes/drains you. Adjust time invested.

Discussion Questions (Group/Book Club)

1. *"Is it fair to expect lifelong friendships in adulthood? Why/why not?"*

2. *How can social media distort our perception of others' friendships?*

Deep Dive (Optional)

Research Spotlight:

- A 2023 *Personality and Social Psychology Review* study found **proximity** predicts friendship survival more than shared history.

Progress Tracker

- Completed "Pillar Check" for 3 friendships.

- Sent one nostalgia text.

- Shared a friendship insight with a group.

Next Steps

- **Read**: *Friendship in the Age of Loneliness* by Adam Smiley Poswolsky.

- **Practice**: Quarterly "friendship audits" using the Three Pillars.

Final Thought: *"Friendships aren't books—they don't need forced endings. Some are meant to be dog-eared and revisited."*

Study Guide & Workbook – Chapter 13

– How to Create the Best Friendships of Your Life

The Proactive Art of Building Meaningful Connections

Summary

This chapter transforms loneliness into action by teaching how to **initiate and nurture adult friendships** through the *Let Me* mindset. The author shares her journey from isolation in a new town to creating deep connections by:

- **"Going First"**: Initiating conversations despite discomfort

- **Building "Weak Ties"**: Cultivating casual connections that strengthen community bonds

- **The One-Year Rule**: Recognizing that meaningful friendships take consistent effort over time

Key Metaphor:

- **"Social Scaffolding"**: Layering connections (from baristas to close friends) to build a supportive network

---

Key Takeaways

1. The "Let Me" Framework for Friendship

Action	Example	Why It Works
Compliment First	"Love your earrings!" to a stranger	Opens dialogue without pressure
Create Contact Notes	"Kevin – tall barista with beard"	Shows intentionality; builds recall
Join Interest-Based Groups	Yoga class → walking club	Leverages the *proximity* pillar

2. The One-Year Rule

- **Reality Check**: Sawyer's college experience shows even extroverts need 12+ months to find their people.

- **Author's Mistake**: Wasted a year self-isolating before knocking on Mia's door.

3. Weak Ties Are Superpowers

- **Research**: Casual connections (like coffee shop regulars) boost belonging (*Journal of Social Psychology*, 2022).

- **Practice**: Learn names of service workers, neighbors, classmates.

Terminology

- **Weak Ties**: Low-stakes relationships that create community fabric (e.g., baristas, gym buddies).

- **Social Scaffolding**: Layered network from acquaintances to close friends.

- **Going First Principle**: Initiating contact to bypass the "waiting to be chosen" trap.

Real-World Applications

1. The 5-Second Introduction

- **Script**: *"Hi, I'm [Name]. New here! How long have you lived/worked/taken this class?"*

- **Tip**: Use context clues (e.g., *"That book looks interesting—what's it about?"*).

2. Interest-Based Connection Plan

1. **Choose 1 activity** (e.g., pottery class, running club).

2. **Attend 3x** before assessing chemistry.

3. **Upgrade 1 connection** to coffee/walk.

3. Digital Contact System

- Create a *"Community"* contact list with descriptors:

"Gregory & Jordan — coffee shop couple from LA. Psychologist + podcaster. Baby Max."

Interactive Workbook

Reflection Prompts

1. **"My Isolation Pattern"**

    o *When have I waited for others to initiate? What did it cost me?*

    o **Your Turn:**_____

2. **Weak Tie Audit**

    o List 5 familiar faces you've never spoken to (e.g., gym regular, librarian).

Analysis Exercise

Case Study: The Walking Group

1. How did the author turn *one* salon connection into a community?

2. What fears might stop someone from starting a similar group?

Application Tasks

1. "Go First" Challenge

- Initiate 3 conversations this week using:

    o A compliment

    o A curiosity question (*"What's that drink you ordered?"*)

    o A shared activity comment (*"This yoga pose kills me too!"*)

2. Friendship Blueprint

- Draft a 3-step plan to meet people:

    1. Join: _____

    2. Initiate: _____

    3. Upgrade: _____

Discussion Questions (Group/Book Club)

1. *"Why do we stigmatize adult friend-seeking but not dating?"*

2. *How can cultural norms make 'going first' harder for some people?*

Deep Dive (Optional)

Research Spotlight:

- A 2023 *Nature Human Behaviour* study found **weak ties** reduce loneliness as effectively as close friends.

Progress Tracker

- Completed 3 "Go First" interactions.
- Joined 1 interest-based group.
- Upgraded 1 connection to a planned meetup.

Next Steps

- **Read**: *The Gifts of Imperfection* by Brené Brown (authentic connection strategies).
- **Practice**: Monthly "friendship audits" using the Three Pillars (Ch. 11).

Final Thought: *"Friendship isn't found—it's forged through the awkward, brave act of reaching out first."*

Study Guide & Workbook – Chapter 14

– People Only Change When They Feel Like It

The Science of Influence and Letting Go

Summary

This chapter dismantles the myth that we can force change in others, revealing why pressure backfires and how to **positively influence** instead. Grounded in neuroscience and psychology, it explains:

- **The Control Paradox**: Pressuring someone triggers their hardwired resistance.

- **The 3 Truths of Change**: Motivation must be internal; humans seek immediate pleasure; everyone thinks they're the exception to risks.

- **The "Let Them" Alternative**: Acceptance creates safety, making change *their* idea.

Key Metaphor:

- **"Swimming Upstream"**: Fighting human nature exhausts you; flow with it instead.

Key Takeaways

I. Why Pressure Fails

Science	Example	"Let Them" Response
Brain's Pleasure Principle	Spouse chooses chips over gym (instant gratification).	*"Let Them enjoy the chips. My nagging only makes the couch stickier."*
Illusion of Exception	Friend believes vaping won't harm *them*.	*"Let Them vape. My warnings are white noise."*
Control Battle	Teen rebels more when told to clean their room.	*"Let Them live in mess. Natural consequences teach better."*

2. The 3 Truths of Change

1. **Internal Motivation Only**: Change happens when *they* feel ready (not when you're ready for them).

2. **Pleasure > Pain**: Humans avoid short-term discomfort (e.g., gym soreness) even for long-term gains.

3. **"It Won't Happen to Me"**: Brains filter out negative warnings (Dr. Sharot's research).

3. The Standoff Cycle

- **Your Move**: Pressure → **Their Move**: Resist → **Result**: Stalemate + resentment.

- **Break It**: Stop pushing. *"Let Them be. Focus on my reactions instead."*

Terminology

- **Agency**: A person's sense of control over their choices (threatened by pressure).

- **Motivation Fallacy**: Believing you can "make" someone want change.

- **Influence vs. Control**: Influence works *with* human nature; control fights it.

Real-World Applications

1. The "No-Sigh" Challenge

- For one week, replace eye rolls/audible sighs with *neutral acceptance* (e.g., "Enjoy your game!"). Observe shifts in tension.

2. Pleasure-Pain Reframe

- For desired changes, ask: *"How could this feel rewarding NOW?"* (e.g., "Gym = podcast time").

3. Agency Audit

- List 3 things you've resisted changing. Note how *others' pressure* affected your motivation.

Interactive Workbook

Reflection Prompts

1. **"My Control Trap"**

   o *Think of someone you've pressured to change. How did they resist? How did it feel?*

   o **Your Turn:**_____

2. **Exception Belief**

   o *What's one "bad habit" you justify as "different" for you? Why?*

Analysis Exercise

Case Study: The Couch Spouse

1. How did the wife's tactics (gifts, sighs) *reduce* her husband's agency?

2. What might happen if she focused on *her* health instead of his?

Application Tasks

1. "Let Them" Journal

- For 3 days, document moments you *want* to pressure someone.

   Write *"Let Them _____ "* instead.

2. Influence Experiment

- Use **autonomy-supportive language**:

   o ✗ "You should workout." → ✓ *"I'm hitting the gym later—love how energized it makes me!"*

Discussion Questions (Group/Book Club)

1. *"When has someone's acceptance (not pressure) inspired you to change?"*

2. *How can cultural norms (e.g., parenting styles) reinforce control battles?*

Deep Dive (Optional)

Research Spotlight:

- A 2022 *Nature Human Behaviour* study found **autonomy-supportive language** increases lasting change by 300% vs. pressure.

Progress Tracker

- Completed 3 "No-Sigh" days.

- Practiced 2 autonomy-supportive phrases.

- Shared one "Exception Belief" with a friend.

Next Steps

- **Read:** *Influencer* by Joseph Grenny (science-backed influence strategies).

- **Practice:** Weekly "agency check" – *"Am I respecting others' autonomy here?"*

Final Thought: *"You can't light a fire with wet wood—no matter how hard you blow. Let Them dry. Tend your own flame."*

Study Guide & Workbook – Chapter 15

– Unlock the Power of Your Influence

The Science of Inspiring Change Without Pressure

Summary

This chapter reveals how to **positively influence** behavior change by leveraging neuroscience and psychology. The author introduces the **ABC Loop** (Apologize-Ask, Back Off, Celebrate) as a research-backed alternative to nagging. Key insights:

- **Social Contagion**: Humans unconsciously mimic behaviors they see working for others (Dr. Sharot's research).

- **Motivational Interviewing**: Open-ended questions help people recognize their own desire for change (Dr. K's technique).

- **The Pleasure Principle**: Immediate positive reinforcement (celebrations!) wires brains to repeat hard actions.

Key Metaphor:

- **"Behavioral Ripples"**: Your actions create waves that influence others' ponds—without a single push.

Key Takeaways

1. Why Influence > Pressure

Pressure Tactics	Why They Fail	Influence Alternative
Nagging about gym time	Triggers resistance	Work out joyfully yourself
Criticizing phone use	Creates defensiveness	Keep your phone in another room
Lecturing about health	Brains tune out warnings	Eat vibrant meals with enthusiasm

2. The ABC Loop

I. **A: Apologize & Ask**

- *"I'm sorry for pressuring you. How do you feel about your health/work habits?"*

- Use **open-ended questions** to spark self-reflection.

2. **B: Back Off**

- Stop monitoring; model the change *without expectation*.

- **Timeline**: 6+ months for organic shifts.

3. **C: Celebrate**

- Immediate positive reinforcement (*"You look energized after that walk!"*) rewires motivation.

3. The 5 Whys Prep Work

- Before the ABC Loop, ask: *"Why does this behavior bother me?"* 5x to uncover your true motivations (e.g., fear, embarrassment, love).

Terminology

- **Social Contagion**: The unconscious adoption of behaviors observed in others.

- **Motivational Interviewing**: A clinical technique using open-ended questions to elicit self-motivation.

- **Intrinsic Motivation**: Internal drive to act (vs. external pressure).

Real-World Applications

1. The "Model & Rave" Technique

- **Do**: Act out desired behaviors *with visible enjoyment* (e.g., *"This salad is so refreshing!"*).

- **Don't**: Comment on their choices.

2. Celebration Inventory

- List 3 tiny wins you can celebrate in others this week (e.g., *"You woke up early—nice discipline!"*).

3. Open-Ended Question Bank

- Prepare 5 neutral questions for tough conversations:

    1. *"What's your perspective on this?"*

    2. *"How do you feel when you [behavior]?"*

Interactive Workbook

Reflection Prompts

1. **"My Pressure Pattern"**

    o *Recall a time you nagged someone. How did they react? What might work better?*

    o **Your Turn**:_____

2. **Influence Map**

    o *Who unconsciously influences YOUR habits? How do they do it?*

Analysis Exercise

Case Study: The Peloton Spouse

1. How did the wife's *initial approach* trigger resistance?

2. How could the ABC Loop rebuild trust?

Application Tasks

1. 5 Whys Drill

- Apply to a frustration: *"Why does my roommate's mess bother me?"* → Dig 5 layers deep.

2. "Stealth Influence" Challenge

- For one week:

    o Model I desired behavior *without commentary*.

o   Celebrate 1 tiny win in someone else.

Discussion Questions (Group/Book Club)

1.   *"When has someone's silent example changed your behavior?"*

2.   *How can power dynamics (parent/child, boss/employee) complicate the ABC Loop?*

Deep Dive (Optional)

Research Spotlight:

- A 2023 *Nature Neuroscience* study found **celebrations** release dopamine, making hard tasks 47% more repeatable.

Progress Tracker

- Completed 5 Whys on one frustration.

- Practiced 3 open-ended questions.

- Noted one "social contagion" observation.

Next Steps

- **Read**: *Change Anything* by Kerry Patterson (science of personal/peer influence).

- **Practice**: Monthly "influence audits" – *"Am I modeling what I seek?"*

Final Thought: *"Be the change you wish to see—then step back and let the ripples reach their shore."*

Study Guide & Workbook – Chapter 16

– The More You Rescue, The More They Sink

The Art of Supportive Non-Intervention

Summary

This chapter confronts the painful paradox of helping: that **over-rescuing often prolongs suffering**. Through neuroscience and clinical research, the author reveals:

- **The Rescue Trap**: Solving others' problems prevents them from developing coping skills.

- **The Brain Science of Struggle**: People only change when avoiding pain becomes harder than facing it.

- **The Football Metaphor**: You can throw the ball (resources), but they must choose to catch it and run.

Key Distinction:

- **Support** = "I'll walk beside you as you face this."

- **Enabling** = "I'll face this for you."

Key Takeaways

1. Why Rescuing Backfires

Rescuing Behavior	Unintended Consequence
Letting an anxious child sleep in your bed	Teaches avoidance over resilience
Giving money to an unemployed adult	Delays financial accountability
Making excuses for an addict	Protects them from rock bottom

2. The Neuroscience of Change

- **Critical Threshold**: Change happens when *staying the same hurts more than changing*.

- **Harvard Research**: Natural consequences (job loss, broken relationships) often motivate better than interventions.

3. The "Let Them" Framework for Support

1. **Validate:** *"I see this is hard for you."*

2. **Separate:** *"Your struggle is not my emergency."*

3. **Empower:** *"You've survived hard things before."*

Terminology

- **Enabling:** Actions that unintentionally perpetuate harmful behaviors.

- **Avoidance Loop:** Chronic evasion of discomfort that worsens anxiety (Dr. Marques' research).

- **Developmental Threshold:** Age 25—when brains are fully equipped for self-regulation.

Real-World Applications

I. The "Support vs. Enable" Audit

- List 3 ways you help someone. Label each:

  ✅ *Support* (builds their capability)

  ✗ *Enable* (removes consequences)

2. Natural Consequences Map

For a loved one's struggle:

1. Short-term consequence they're avoiding: _____

2. Long-term benefit of facing it: _____

3. The "Football Play"

Next time they ask for help:

- *Throw the ball:* "Here's a therapist's number."

- *Don't run it:* Don't book the appointment for them.

Interactive Workbook

Reflection Prompts

1. **"My Rescue Instinct"**

    o   *When has "helping" someone actually kept them stuck?*

    o   **Your Turn:**_____

2. **Anxiety Avoidance Journal**

    o   Recall a time you avoided discomfort. How did it affect you long-term?

Analysis Exercise

Case Study: The Anxious Daughter

1. How did the author's nightly rescues reinforce the anxiety cycle?

2. What healthier alternative aligned with Dr. Marques' research?

Application Tasks

1. "Support Script" Practice

- Roleplay these responses:

    o   *"I believe you can handle this."*

    o   *"What's one small step you could take?"*

2. Boundary Blueprint

- For one enabling pattern:

    o   My current behavior: _____

    o   My new boundary: _____

Discussion Questions (Group/Book Club)

1. *"Where is the line between compassion and codependency?"*

2. *How can cultural/family expectations make 'non-rescuing' harder?*

Deep Dive (Optional)

Research Spotlight:

- A 2023 *Journal of Clinical Psychology* study found **natural consequences** motivate change 3x more than interventions.

Progress Tracker

- Completed "Support vs. Enable" audit.

- Practiced 2 "support scripts."

- Set 1 new boundary.

Next Steps

- **Read**: *Codependent No More* by Melody Beattie (breaking rescue cycles).

- **Practice**: Weekly "football checks"—*"Did I throw the ball or run it for them?"*

Final Thought: *"Rescuing says, 'You're fragile.' Supporting says, 'You're formidable.' Choose your message wisely."*

Study Guide & Workbook – Chapter 17

– How to Provide Support the Right Way

The Art of Empowered Helping

Summary

This chapter reframes support from *rescuing* to *empowering*, offering concrete strategies to help loved ones without enabling dependency. Key distinctions include:

- **Financial Leverage**: Money given *with conditions* is support; *without conditions* is enabling.

- **Environmental Healing**: Creating spaces/rituals that make recovery easier (e.g., meal drops, activity invites).

- **The Rock Bottom Paradox**: Sometimes withdrawal of support is the ultimate act of love.

Key Metaphor:

- **"Scaffolding vs. Crutch"**: Temporary support structures vs. permanent dependencies.

Key Takeaways

1. Financial Boundaries That Work

Enabling	Empowering Support
Paying rent unconditionally	*"I'll cover rent if you attend weekly therapy."*
Endless "loans" with no plan	*"I'll pay for job training—here are 3 programs to choose from."*
Ignoring broken agreements	*"No more car payments until you're sober for 30 days."*

2. The 3 Pillars of Environmental Support

1. **Physical Space**: Clean homes, healthy meals, open curtains (literally and metaphorically).

2. **Social Connection**: *"I'm picking you up for yoga every Wednesday—no need to reply."*

3. **Ritual Anchors**: Pre-scheduled outings to rebuild routine.

3. Non-Transactional Helping

- **Do**: Drop off dinner without expecting thanks.

- **Don't**: Keep score of who "owes" what.

Terminology

- **Conditional Support**: Resources tied to accountability (e.g., therapy attendance).

- **Environmental Healing**: Curating physical/social spaces that foster recovery.

- **Rock Bottom Moment**: When the helper (not just the struggler) hits their limit.

Real-World Applications

1. The "Contract Method"

- Draft a *support agreement* with a loved one:

  "I will _____ if you _____. We'll reassess monthly."

2. Environmental Audit

For someone struggling:

- **Barrier**: Cluttered bedroom → **Support**: Offer to help organize.

- **Barrier**: Isolation → **Support**: Weekly podcast walk-and-talks.

3. The "No-Ask Help" Challenge

- For one month, provide 3 concrete assists *without being asked* (e.g., laundry, grocery runs).

Interactive Workbook

Reflection Prompts

1. **"My Rescue Tendencies"**

    o *What's one situation where I crossed from helping to enabling? What boundary did I need?*

    o **Your Turn:**_____

2. **Conditional Compassion**

    o *Why might "I love you too much to fund your avoidance" be kinder than blank checks?*

Analysis Exercise

Case Study: Chris's Business Crisis

1. How did his brother's refusal to loan money *accelerate* positive change?

2. What enabled behaviors might have prolonged the struggle?

Application Tasks

1. Support Blueprint

- For a loved one:

    o I financial boundary: _____

    o I environmental tweak: _____

    o I no-ask help: _____

2. "Thank-Free Giving" Experiment

- Perform one kind act *without expecting acknowledgment.* Note how it feels.

Discussion Questions (Group/Book Club)

1. *"How can cultural norms about family obligation clash with healthy boundaries?"*

2. *When does 'tough love' become cruelty? Where's the line?*

Deep Dive (Optional)

Research Spotlight:

- A 2023 *Journal of Family Psychology* study found **conditional financial support** led to 5x faster recovery rates in addiction cases.

Progress Tracker

- Drafted one support agreement.

- Completed environmental audit.

- Performed one thank-free act of support.

Next Steps

- **Read**: *Set Boundaries, Find Peace* by Nedra Glover Tawwab.

- **Practice**: Quarterly "support check-ins" to reassess conditions.

Final Thought: *"True support hands someone a flashlight—not a carried weight."*

Study Guide & Workbook – Chapter 18

– Let Them Show You Who They Are

Summary

This chapter explores the complexities of love, dating, and relationships through the lens of the **"Let Them Theory"**—a philosophy that emphasizes observing others' behavior rather than chasing or manipulating outcomes. Key themes include:

- The power of self-worth in love.

- The dangers of chasing potential instead of accepting reality.

- How to differentiate between mutual effort and one-sided relationships.

- The importance of letting people reveal their true intentions through actions.

Key Takeaways

1. Love Should Be Mutual, Not Chased

- **Chasing love** often leads to settling for less than you deserve.

- **Choosing love** means recognizing when someone actively chooses you back.

- **Example:** If you're always initiating texts/plans, you're chasing—not being chosen.

2. Behavior Reveals True Intentions

- Words can lie; actions don't.

  o   Mixed signals = disinterest.

  o   Consistent effort = genuine investment.

- **Analogy:** A job applicant who says they're "excited" but never shows up isn't serious.

3. Dating Is a Process of Elimination

- The goal isn't just to find "The One" but to **learn** what you truly want.

- Every failed relationship teaches you about your boundaries and dealbreakers.

4. Self-Respect Over Fantasy

- Avoid romanticizing potential—accept reality.

- **Signs you're in denial:**

    o   Making excuses for poor treatment.

    o   Believing "they'll change."

    o   Confusing chemistry for compatibility.

5. The "Let Them Theory" in Action

- **Let Them:** Ghost you, confuse you, show disinterest.

- **Let Me:** Walk away, uphold standards, focus on reciprocity.

Terminology

- **Let Them Theory:** Allowing others' actions (not words) to guide your decisions.

- **Situationship:** A relationship lacking clear commitment or labels.

- **Mutual Effort:** Balanced investment from both partners.

- **Chasing Love:** Pursuing someone who isn't equally engaged.

Real-World Applications

1. **Audit Your Relationships:**

    o   List the last 3 people you dated. Did they match your effort?

2. **Behavior Journal:**

    o   Track actions (e.g., canceled plans, vague replies) for 2 weeks.

3. **The "Friend Test":**

o   Ask: *"Would I let my best friend accept this treatment?"*

Interactive Workbook

Reflection Prompts

1. **Your Turn:** *Write about a time you chased potential. What did you ignore?*

2. **Let Me Challenge:** *What's one relationship habit you need to stop justifying?*

Analysis Exercises

Case Study: *Alex texts you daily but never makes plans. Using the Let Them Theory, what would you conclude?*

- **A)** They're shy but interested.

- **B)** They enjoy attention but aren't serious.

- **C)** They're busy; be patient.

    (Answer: B – Behavior shows low priority.)

Application Tasks

1. **Clean Break:** Delete/archive contacts who've shown disinterest.

2. **Boundary Script:** Practice saying: *"I'm looking for consistency. If that's not you, no hard feelings."*

Discussion Questions (Group/Book Club)

- How has social media/dating apps distorted modern love?

- Why is it hard to accept when someone isn't interested?

Professional Enhancements

Bloom's Taxonomy Scaffolding

- **Remember:** List 3 signs of one-sided effort.

- **Analyze:** Compare a past relationship to the Let Them Theory.

- **Create:** Draft a "relationship standards" manifesto.

Deep Dive (Optional)

- **Attachment Styles:** How does your style (anxious/avoidant) affect dating choices?

Progress Tracker

- Week 1: Identify 1 chase pattern.

- Week 2: Set 1 new boundary.

Next Steps

- **Read:** *Attached* by Amir Levine (on attachment theory).

- **Try:** A 30-day "no chasing" challenge.

Final Note: Love isn't about winning someone over—it's about finding someone who *chooses* you as you are. Let them.

Study Guide & Workbook – Chapter 19

– How to Take Your Relationship to the Next Level

Summary

This chapter tackles the challenge of **uncommitted relationships** and how to navigate the "commitment conversation" using the **Let Them Theory**. Key themes include:

- Breaking patterns of chasing emotionally unavailable partners.

- The importance of self-work (therapy, intentional singleness) to break cycles.

- How to frame a **powerful, non-needy commitment conversation**.

- Accepting rejection gracefully and valuing your time.

Key Takeaways

I. Are You Stuck in a Commitment-Phobe Pattern?

- **Signs you chase unavailability:**

  o Dating people who "won't label it," cheat, or need "rescuing."

  o Believing you're the "exception" who can change them.

- **Research-backed truth:**

  o University of Alberta study shows we **repeat relationship dynamics** from past trauma.

  o Solution: **Be single** to break the cycle.

2. The "Let Them Theory" for Commitment

- **Let Them:** Avoid labels, delay milestones, or reject commitment.

- **Let Me:** Walk away, invest time wisely, and seek reciprocity.

- **Analogy:** Staying with a non-committal partner is like **ordering a 5-star meal but accepting table scraps**.

3. How to Have the Commitment Conversation

- **Matthew Hussey's script (non-needy framework):**
  - ○ Focus on **your standards**, not their flaws.
  - ○ Example: *"I value my time and only invest in relationships moving toward commitment."*
- **Avoid:** Emotional pleas, ultimatums, or vague hints.

4. Acceptance Over Denial

- If they refuse commitment: **Their behavior is the answer.**
- **Painful but freeing truth:** Rejection redirects you to better matches.

Terminology

- **Commitment-phobe:** A partner who avoids labels/exclusivity despite intimacy.
- **Trauma repetition:** Unconsciously recreating past dysfunctional dynamics.
- **Non-needy framing:** Asserting needs without desperation (e.g., Hussey's script).

Real-World Applications

1. **Pattern Audit:** List your last 3 partners. Did they avoid commitment? What's the common thread?
2. **Therapy Prompt:** Explore childhood/family models that normalized unavailability.
3. **Script Practice:** Role-play the commitment conversation with a friend.

Interactive Workbook

Reflection Prompts

1. **Your Turn:** *Write about a time you ignored red flags to "keep" someone. What did it cost you?*

2. **Let Me Challenge:** *What's one commitment-related fear you need to confront?*

Analysis Exercises

Case Study: *Taylor has dated Alex for 6 months. Alex says "I love you" but avoids meeting friends or labeling the relationship. Using the Let Them Theory, what should Taylor do?*

- **A)** Give an ultimatum.

- **B)** Use Hussey's script to clarify intentions.

- **C)** Wait longer; Alex just needs time.

   (Answer: B – Behavior reveals priorities; clarity is key.)

Application Tasks

1. **"Table Scraps" Journal:** List compromises you've made in past relationships. Would you accept them now?

2. **Boundary Blueprint:** Draft your "non-negotiables" for future commitments (e.g., exclusivity timelines).

Discussion Questions (Group/Book Club)

- Why do people fear being single more than being stuck in unfulfilling relationships?

- How can societal pressure (e.g., "marriage timelines") distort our commitment choices?

Professional Enhancements

Bloom's Taxonomy Scaffolding

- **Remember:** Define "trauma repetition" in your own words.

- **Evaluate:** Compare Hussey's script to traditional ultimatums. Which fosters mutual respect?

- **Create:** Design a "relationship timeline" aligning with your personal goals.

Deep Dive (Optional)

- **Attachment Styles:** How does an **anxious attachment** fuel commitment-chasing?

Progress Tracker

- Week 1: Identify 1 past relationship pattern.

- Week 2: Practice Hussey's script (even hypothetically).

Next Steps

- **Read:** *Mr. Unavailable and the Fallback Girl* (on emotional unavailability).

- **Try:** A 3-month "dating detox" to reset patterns.

Final Note: Commitment isn't something you extract—it's something **freely given**. Let their actions guide you.

Study Guide & Workbook – Chapter 20

– How Every Ending Is a Beautiful Beginning

Summary

This chapter explores **relationship endings, compatibility, and heartbreak** through the lens of the **Let Them Theory**. Key themes include:

- Differentiating between **solvable problems** and **fundamental incompatibilities**.

- The **ABC(DE) Loop** for evaluating relationships: Apologize, Back off, Celebrate progress, Decide (deal breaker?), End (bitching or relationship).

- Navigating **heartbreak** with neuroscience-backed strategies.

- Recognizing that **self-love** is the foundation of all healthy relationships.

Key Takeaways

1. Is Your Relationship Worth Saving?

- **Two requirements for long-term success:**

    1. **Both partners** want it to work **and** are willing to put in effort.

    2. The issues **don't require sacrificing core values or dreams.**

- **Gottman Research:** 69% of relationship conflicts are **unsolvable** (e.g., personality differences).

- **Ask:** *"Can I accept them exactly as they are forever?"* If not, it may be a **deal breaker.**

2. The ABC(DE) Loop for Tough Decisions

- **A (Apologize & Ask):** Address issues kindly. *"I've been frustrated about X. How do you see it?"*

- **B (Back Off & Behavior):** Observe their actions for **3 months**. Do they try?

- C (Celebrate Change): Reinforce positive shifts. *"I noticed you did X—thank you!"*

- D (Decide): Is this a **deal breaker**? *"Could I live with this forever?"*

- E (End): End your complaining or **end the relationship**. No middle ground.

3. Compatibility vs. Commitment

- **Commitment ≠ Compatibility.** You can love someone deeply but want different futures (e.g., kids, location).

- **Test for deal breakers:**

  o *"Will I regret losing them more than sacrificing my dream?"*

  o *"If nothing changes in 5 years, will I be happy?"*

4. Surviving Heartbreak (Neuroscience-Backed Tips)

- **No contact for 30 days** (resets nervous system attachments).

- **Remove triggers:** Photos, gifts, social media.

- **Rebuild routines:** Redecorate your space, take a class, travel.

- **Time doesn't heal—action does.** 71% feel better by 11 weeks (research).

5. You Are the Love of Your Life

- **Relationships mirror self-worth.** The **Let Them Theory** starts with *"Let Me"*:

  o *Let Me set boundaries.*

  o *Let Me walk away from disrespect.*

  o *Let Me choose happiness.*

Terminology

- **Deal breaker:** A non-negotiable need (e.g., wanting kids, fidelity).

- **Trauma bonding:** Staying due to emotional highs/lows, not love.

- **Nervous system reset:** Detaching from an ex's psychological "imprint."

Real-World Applications

1. **Deal Breaker List:** Write 3 absolute needs for future relationships.

2. **ABC(DE) Practice:** Apply the loop to a current/past relationship issue.

3. **Post-Breakup Plan:** Schedule one self-care activity per week (e.g., therapy, hiking).

Interactive Workbook

Reflection Prompts

1. **Your Turn:** *Recall a relationship that ended. Did you ignore incompatibilities? Why?*

2. **Let Me Challenge:** *What's one dream you'd never sacrifice for a partner?*

Analysis Exercises

Case Study: *Jamie loves Alex but Alex refuses to move for Jamie's dream job. Using the ABC(DE) Loop, what should Jamie do?*

*   **A)** Give an ultimatum.

*   **B)** Accept Alex's stance and decide: stay or leave.

*   **C)** *(Answer: B – "Let Them" reveal priorities, then "Let Me" choose self-respect.)*

Application Tasks

1. **"Clean Break" Checklist:**

    o   Delete ex's number.

    o   Box up mementos.

    o   Plan a post-breakup trip.

2. **Script Writing:** Draft a tough conversation using the **ABC steps**.

Discussion Questions (Group/Book Club)

- How can societal pressure (e.g., "marriage by 30") cloud judgment on compatibility?

- Why is "staying for the kids" often harmful long-term?

Professional Enhancements

Bloom's Taxonomy Scaffolding

- **Remember:** List Gottman's two relationship requirements.

- **Evaluate:** Compare a past breakup to the ABC(DE) Loop. What would you do differently?

- **Create:** Design a "relationship values" vision board.

Deep Dive (Optional)

- **Attachment Science:** How does an **anxious attachment** prolong unhealthy relationships?

Progress Tracker

- Week 1: Identify 1 deal breaker.

- Week 2: Practice the **"Back Off"** step in a conflict.

Next Steps

- **Read:** *The Breakup Bible* (on heartbreak recovery).

- **Try:** A **"Let Me" 30-day challenge** (e.g., saying no to people-pleasing).

Final Note: Endings aren't failures—they're **redirects** to love that aligns. Let go with grace.

Study Guide & Workbook – Conclusion

– Your Let Me Era Is Here

Summary

This powerful conclusion reframes the **Let Them Theory** as a philosophy for **personal empowerment**. Key themes:

- The realization that **you—not others—control your happiness and responses.**

- How **releasing the need to control external factors** (people, circumstances) frees you to focus on **what you can control.**

- A call to action: **Step into your "Let Me Era"**—where you take ownership of your dreams, boundaries, and life.

Key Takeaways

1. The Sky Analogy: Accepting What You Can't Control

- **People and situations = weather.** You can't stop storms (others' actions), but you **choose your response** (carry an umbrella, dance in the rain).

- **Example:** A rude comment is a "cloud." You decide if it ruins your day (*giving power away*) or rolls off (*keeping power*).

2. The Cost of Not Using "Let Them" and "Let Me"

- **Let Them Failure:** Wasting energy resisting reality (e.g., waiting for validation, resenting others' success).

- **Let Me Failure:** Missing opportunities due to fear (not applying for the dream job, stifling creativity).

- **Question:** *What have you sacrificed by focusing on others instead of yourself?*

3. Reclaiming Your Power

- **Stop:** People-pleasing, rescuing, chasing love, fearing opinions.

- **Start:** Protecting peace, pursuing goals unapologetically, choosing mutual relationships.

- **Mantra:** *"I am responsible for my happiness. No one owes me anything—but I owe myself everything."*

4. The "Let Me Era" Begins Now

- **"Let Me" is active ownership:**
  - *Let Me set boundaries.*
  - *Let Me take the first step.*
  - *Let Me believe in my dreams.*

- **Liberation:** When you stop letting others dictate your worth, **everything becomes possible.**

Terminology

- **Let Them Theory:** Allowing others to be who they are while **choosing your response.**

- **Let Me Era:** A mindset shift to **self-accountability** and purposeful action.

- **Nervous system reset:** Detaching from external validation (tied to heartbreak/healing).

Real-World Applications

1. **Power Audit:** List 3 areas where you've given away control (e.g., over-explaining to critics). How can you reclaim it?

2. **"Let Me" Goals:** Choose one bold action to take this week (e.g., *Let Me pitch my idea*).

3. **Weather Journal:** For a week, note "storms" (external chaos) and how you navigated them.

Interactive Workbook

Reflection Prompts

1. **Your Turn:** *What's one dream you've delayed due to fear of others' opinions?*

2. **Let Me Challenge:** *Write a letter to your future self about the life you're choosing to create.*

Analysis Exercises

Case Study: *Sam wants to start a business but fears family judgment. Using the sky analogy, what's their path forward?*

- **A)** Wait for family approval.

- **B)** Start small, accept some may disapprove (*Let Them*), and focus on progress (*Let Me*).

- **C)** Abandon the idea to avoid conflict.

   (Answer: B – "Let Them" have opinions; "Let Me" build anyway.)

Application Tasks

1. **Boundary Scripts:**

   o *"I appreciate your concern, but I'm trusting my gut on this."*

   o *"I can't fix this for you, but I'm here to listen."*

2. **"Let Me" Vision Board:** Collage images representing your unapologetic goals.

Discussion Questions (Group/Book Club)

- How does social media make it harder to embrace the *Let Them* mindset?

- Share a time you took back power. How did it feel?

Professional Enhancements

Bloom's Taxonomy Scaffolding

- **Remember:** Define "Let Me Era" in your own words.

- **Analyze:** Compare a past "people-pleasing" moment to how you'd handle it now.

- **Create:** Draft a "Let Me Manifesto" (5 personal commandments).

Deep Dive (Optional)

- **Cognitive Dissonance:** Why do we cling to control even when it harms us?

Progress Tracker

- Week 1: Practice saying *"Let Them"* in one frustrating situation.

- Week 2: Take one *"Let Me"* action toward a dream.

Next Steps

- **Read:** *The Subtle Art of Not Giving a Fck** (on prioritization).

- **Try:** A **"No Explanation" Week** (stop justifying personal choices).

Final Note: The *Let Me Era* isn't selfish—it's **self-honoring**. The world needs your unedited voice.

Loved the Book? Let the World Know! ✹

You've just unlocked powerful tools to reclaim your peace and power—**now it's your turn to spread the magic!**

📖 Did *The Let Them Theory* shift your mindset?

💬 Did a particular lesson hit home?

✦ Are you stepping into your *"Let Me Era"* with newfound confidence?

Drop a review and let others discover this life-changing read! Your words could be the nudge someone needs to start their own transformation.

☞ Tap those stars ★ ★ ★ ★ ★ and share your takeaway!

(Even a line or two makes a world of difference.)

Manufactured by Amazon.ca
Acheson, AB

16618478R00050